# Around the World
# Schools

Margaret C. Hall

**Heinemann Library**
Chicago, Illinois

© 2002 Reed Educational & Professional Publishing
Published by Heinemann Library,
an imprint of Reed Educational & Professional Publishing,
Chicago, Illinois

Customer Service 888-454-2279
Visit our website at www.heinemannlibrary.com

Designed by Lisa Buckley
Printed in Hong Kong

06 05 04 03 02
10 9 8 7 6 5 4 3 2 1

**Library of Congress Cataloging-in-Publication Data**
Hall, Margaret, 1947-
  Schools / Margaret Hall.
      p. cm. -- (Around the world)
Includes bibliographical references and index.
Summary: Presents an overview of the world's schools with their various customs, curriculum, and activities, as well as school transportation and clothing.
  ISBN 1-58810-477-X (lib. bdg.)
  1. Schools--Juvenile literature. 2. Students--Juvenile literature.
[1. Schools. 2. Students.] I. Title.
  LB1513 .H35 2002
  371--dc21

                         2001002471

**Acknowledgments**
The author and publishers are grateful to the following for permission to reproduce copyright material:

Cover photograph reproduced with permission of Earl and Nazima Kowell/Corbis

Title page, p.10 Sovfoto/Eastfoto/PictureQuest; p.4 © Wolfgang Kaehler; p.5 Michael Dwyer—Stock, Boston, Inc./PictureQuest; p.6 John Elk/Stock, Boston; p.7 © Nik Wheeler; p.8 Helga Lade/Peter Arnold, Inc.; p.9 Jacques Jangoux—Stock Connection/PictureQuest; p.11 Bill Bachmann/The Image Works; p.12 Mark Edwards—Still Pictures/Peter Arnold, Inc.; p.13 Jeff Greenberg/Peter Arnold, Inc.; p.14 Shehzad Noorani—Still Pictures/Peter Arnold, Inc.; p.15, Bob Daemmrich/Stock, Boston, Inc.; p.16 David Klammer/The Image Works; p.17 Lionel Coates/Bruce Coleman Inc.; p.18 Elizabeth Crews/The Image Works; p.19 Michael Wolf—Visum/The Image Works; p.20 Dean Conger/Corbis; p.21 Paul A. Souders/Corbis; p.22 South American Pictures; p.23 J. Schytte—Still Pictures/Peter Arnold, Inc.; p.24 James Marshall/The Image Works; p.25 Bob Daemmrich/The Image Works; p.26 © Victor Englebert; p.27 Ken Heyman/Woodfin Camp and Associates; p.28 Don L. Boroughs/The Image Works; p.29 Howard Davies/Corbis

Every effort has been made to contact copyright holders of any material reproduced in this book. Any omissions will be rectified in subsequent printings if notice is given to the publisher.

The author would like to thank her family—John, Alison, and Jason.

Some words are shown in bold, **like this.** You can find out what they mean by looking in the glossary.

# Contents

# Schools Around the World

This classroom is in Alor Island, Indonesia.

All around the world, children go to school. Some children spend most of their day at school. Others spend only a few hours there.

These girls in Chile are leaving their school for the day.

Schools are different in different parts of the world. But they are all the same in one way. Schools are where children go to learn.

# School Buildings

This large school building is in Thailand.

The kind of school buildings children have depends on where they live. It depends on the **climate** and the **resources** of their community.

Some children in Pakistan go to school outside.

School buildings can be large or small. They can be made from many different materials. Some children even go to school outside or in buildings with no walls.

# Getting to School

These North Korean children are walking to school.

Children travel to school in many different ways. The kind of **transportation** they use depends on where they live. It also depends on how far they have to go.

Some boys in Zaire travel to school by boat on the Ngiri River.

Many children walk or ride bicycles to school. Others ride in cars, on buses, or on a train. Some children go to school by boat.

# School Clothing

These boys in Mongolia wear warm clothes to walk to school in the snow.

Children around the world wear different kinds of clothing to school. What they wear often depends on the **climate** where they live. It also depends on what **season** it is.

Many children in China wear school uniforms.

In some schools, the **students** all dress alike. They wear **uniforms.** Students from different schools have different uniforms.

# The School Day

These children in Cameroon are studying in a small group.

All around the world, teachers help **students** learn new things. Children do some schoolwork in groups. They do other schoolwork on their own.

Students in France may go with their teacher on a field trip to see a cathedral, or large church.

Most children eat lunch or a snack at school. They may also have time to play. At many schools, children take class trips, too.

# Learning to Read and Write

A teacher in Bangladesh helps two of her students with their writing.

One important job for teachers is to help children learn to read and write. **Students** learn to read and write in many different **languages.**

A second-grade girl in Mexico is studying English.

The language children use at school depends on where they live. Some children study their own language and another language, too.

# Other Lessons

A boy in India is getting help with his math from his teacher.

Children learn many things at school. All around the world, they study math and science. They learn about their own country and other countries, too.

British students may take music lessons at school.

Many children around the world study art and music in school. They may also learn how to use a computer.

# School Chores

This young girl is helping to set up her Spanish classroom in California.

Most children have **chores** to do at school. They help to keep the classroom neat and clean. They may even help to set up the classroom every day.

Children in Japan help serve lunch to their classmates.

In some places, children work to keep the schoolyard neat and clean. Some children may serve lunch to one another.

# After School

A tutor helps a Mongolian girl with her reading.

Some children go to school even after the school day is over. They may have a **tutor** to help them with the subjects that are harder for them.

A seven-year-old girl in Ireland studies Hebrew.

Some children have other lessons after school. They study things they cannot learn in school. They may learn about dance, music, or their own **culture.**

# Special Schools

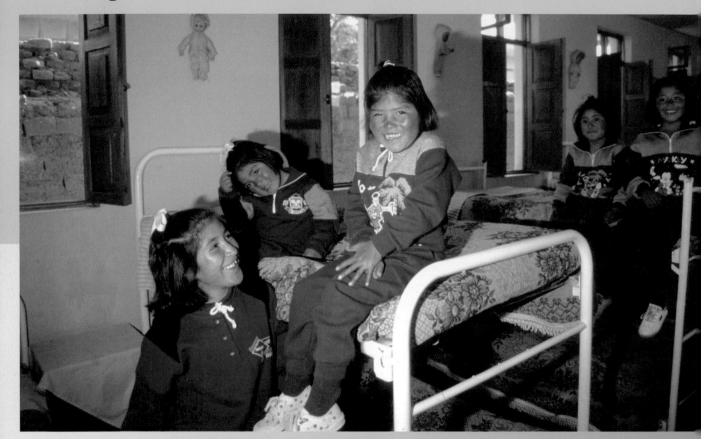

These girls in Peru live at their school.

Some children live at their schools. These schools are called **boarding schools.** The children go home for visits and on holidays.

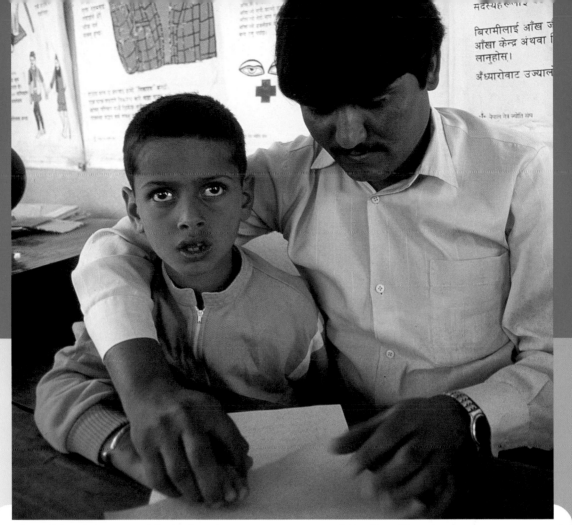

This blind boy in Nepal is learning to read in Braille.

This boy is **blind.** He goes to a school where he can learn to read and write in a special way. People who are blind read with their fingers. They use a system of raised dots called **Braille.**

# Home Schooling

This mother in Maine teaches her three children at home.

A home can also be a school. Some parents teach their children at home. They want to decide exactly what their children will learn.

Students who learn at home may go to a school to use a gym.

People at schools will often help parents plan home lessons for their children. Many children who study at home go to a school for gym or art classes.

# School and Work

This young girl in Peru sells gum and candy to help earn money for her family.

In some places, children must help their families earn money. They go to school for only part of the day. Then they work for part of the day.

These girls are studying geography together at a Russian school for ballerinas.

Some children work as **performers.** They spend part of their day **practicing** the work that they do. They spend the rest of the day studying regular school subjects.

# Older Students

These college students in South Africa are studying engineering.

Many people go to school even after they are **adults.** They may go to **college.** Or, they may go to a **trade school** to learn how to do a certain job.

These women in India are in a language class for adults.

Adults also take classes for fun. They study different **languages** and learn how to do things. No matter how old **students** are, they go to school to learn.

# Amazing School Facts

⭐ In some places, children live too far away from their school to go there. Teachers give lessons over the radio or by using computers that are hooked up to the school.

⭐ One of the subjects that was taught in ancient Greece was gymnastics. They thought gymnastics was just as important to learn as math or reading!

⭐ Schools have been around for thousands of years. The first schools were started to teach children about their **culture.**

⭐ A long time ago, a German man started a new kind of school. He thought that small children should grow like flowers in a garden. He called his school *kindergarten.* The word means "children's garden" in German.

# Glossary

**adult** grown-up person

**blind** cannot see

**boarding school** school where children also live

**Braille** system of raised dots used as an alphabet for people who cannot see

**chore** small job

**climate** normal type of weather for an area

**college** school for older students

**culture** belief system and ways of doing things among a certain group

**language** system of words people use to speak, write, and read

**performer** someone such as a dancer or actor who entertains others

**practice** to do something over and over to get better at it

**resource** something available for people to use

**season** time of the year

**student** someone who goes to a school to learn

**trade school** school where people learn how to do a certain job

**transportation** ways people move from place to place

**tutor** teacher who works with a student or small group outside of the classroom

**uniform** clothing that shows that a person goes to a certain school

# More Books to Read

Kalman, Bobbie. *School from A to Z.* New York: Crabtree, 1999.

Roop, Peter. *A School Album.* Chicago: Heinemann Library, 1999.

Steele, Philip. *Going to School.* Danbury, Conn.: Franklin Watts, 2000.

# Index